THE
LITTLE YOGHURT
BOOK

Elizabeth Cornish

PIATKUS

© 1987 Judy Piatkus (Publishers) Limited

First published in 1987 by
Judy Piatkus (Publishers) Limited,
5 Windmill Street, London W1

British Library Cataloguing in Publication Data
Cornish, Elizabeth
   The little yoghurt book.
   1. Yoghurt
   I. Title
   637'.146   SF275.Y6

   ISBN 0-86188-616-X

Drawings by Hanife Hassan
Designed by Sue Ryall
Cover illustrated by Lynne Robinson

Phototypeset in Linotron Plantin by
Phoenix Photosetting, Chatham
Printed and bound in Great Britain by
The Bath Press, Avon

CONTENTS

WHAT IS YOGHURT?

Yoghurt is believed to have originated in the Balkans and Eastern Mediterranean countries. One bizarre theory is that it was first discovered by the nomadic tribes wandering the Sahara who carried milk in bags made from the stomachs of slaughtered animals. The action of the sun and the bacteria already in the 'bag' would have turned the milk into a surprisingly palatable solid – yoghurt.

According to one legend, it was Noah who first made yoghurt on a large scale. While the Ark was floating on the Flood, his animals produced more milk than he knew what to do with. He stored this excess milk in bags made of animals' stomachs, and yoghurt was the result.

It is impossible to be specific about when yoghurt first became a recognised food, but it is recorded that the Pharaohs ate it at their banquets. In all probability, since yoghurt is the natural product of leaving milk standing under certain conditions, it has been enjoyed all over the world for as long as milk has been drunk.

Once the conditions for making yoghurt had been recognised, methods were developed to produce it by design, rather than by accident. Traditionally it was made from the milk of cows, ewes or goats by a method of prolonged boiling in open pans. This concentrated the milk, increasing the milk solids content by more than a third. The concentrated milk was allowed to cool, then a small quantity of yoghurt from a previously made batch was stirred in. The bacteria multiplied, producing enough lactic acid to sour and coagulate the milk, and yoghurt was formed.

Yoghurt was eaten by the prophets of the Old Testament. Job 10:10 says: *'Hast thou not poured me out as milk, and curdled me like cheese?'*

YOGHURT IN THE MIDDLE EAST

The name 'yoghurt' is Armenian, from the Indo-European words *yough* (oil) and *guard* (curd). So yoghurt was the oil of the curd, or in other words, the whey. The present day Armenian word for yoghurt, *matzoon*, is derived from the Sanskrit *mast*, which means curdled milk.

In Armenian folklore, *mast* was ambrosia – it made the gods immortal and filled men with strength and vigour. The supreme deity was called 'Ara-mast', 'all-powerful Masta', and shows the high regard accorded to the powers of yoghurt!

When the Armenian tribes were dispersed by Arab and then Turkish invaders, they wandered as far as Rumania in the west and India in the east, taking their magic food with them. About 3,000 years ago the yogis of India, who were descended from the original Armenians, laid down rules of healthy eating and drinking in the Vedas, which advised their followers to abstain from eating all sour foods, with one exception, yoghurt, which they referred to as 'the food of the gods'.

In Middle Eastern households to this day, the making of yoghurt goes on side by side with the baking of bread. As the culture from one batch is used as the starter for the next and yoghurt is taken by emigrants to new countries and by brides to new homes, yoghurt can truly be said to be eternal, justifying its reputation as the food of the gods.

YOGHURT AS A HEALTH FOOD

Yoghurt is deservedly regarded as a health food because its lactic acid content prevents the growth of harmful organisms, especially those responsible for gastro-intestinal infections. It is a good source of protein and other nutrients derived from milk.

It was the Russian bacteriologist E. Metchnikoff who introduced yoghurt to western Europe, where its popularity spread quickly, and is still on the increase. In 1907 he published a book called *The Prolongation of Life*, in which he claimed that the extraordinary health and longevity of the Balkan peasants whose lifestyle he had studied was due to the effects of certain bacteria in the large quantities of yoghurt they ate. He believed that *Lactobacillus bulgaricus*, the main species of bacteria present in yoghurt, was capable of multiplying and destroying harmful bacteria in the bowel. Research has since proved that *L. bulgaricus* does not multiply in the bowel, but yoghurt and long life continue to be linked in the minds of many yoghurt eaters.

THE WORK OF PROFESSOR METCHNIKOFF

Professor Metchnikoff (1845–1916), in his research at the Pasteur Institute in Paris, was the first person to isolate the two types of bacillus that turn milk into yoghurt. They are *Streptococcus thermophilus* and *Lactobacillus bulgaricus*, which is very similar to the digestive bacteria in an unweaned baby's intestines.

When the baby is introduced to solid foods, the bacteria in its intestines increase accordingly in number and variety. If the child is fed on a healthy diet, the bacteria will largely resemble the original organisms produced by a milk diet. But if the diet is excessively rich in meat, or too heavy on carbohydrates, then harmful bacteria form and begin to contaminate the system.

Armed with his knowledge about the health and longevity of the Balkan peasants and the above information, Metchnikoff researched into the uses of yoghurt as a purgative. In his book he reports that an Italian doctor called Rovighi, who shared his beliefs, experimented by drinking 1.5 litres of *kefir* a day over a period of several days, and testing his urine for toxins before and afterwards. *Kefir* is a liquid type of yoghurt made in Russia and it contains 3% alcohol. Rovighi found that drinking it cleared his body of poisons.

Metchnikoff disapproved of the alcoholic content of *kefir*, but he said that eating yoghurt regularly would keep the system so pure that a man could live

for 150 years. Unfortunately he himself died at the age of 71, only half the age he hoped to reach.

One of the problems with Metchnikoff's own diet was that his keenness for yoghurt led him to believe that all food should have its smooth consistency. He advised against eating raw fruit and vegetables, recommending that everything should be thoroughly cooked, sterilised and pulverised. Sadly, he did not realise that roughage, in the form of vegetable fibre, was essential for healthy digestion. His researches were also carried out before the discovery of vitamins, which did not take place until 1919.

Eventually Metchnikoff's obsession with the harmful bacteria in the large intestine led him to advocate its removal by surgery! Nevertheless, it is largely due to his work that yoghurt is so widely enjoyed in Europe today.

OTHER FAMOUS CHAMPIONS OF YOGHURT

The Bulgarians have always believed that they owed their health and long life to eating yoghurt. Before the last war, Bulgaria had only eight million inhabitants, yet it boasted more centenarians than the United States. Bulgarian yoghurt is thick and acidic, and sometimes even alcoholic.

In fact it has been known for many centuries that yoghurt promotes health. In 633 a book called *The Great Explanation of the Power of the Elements and Medicine* was published in Damascus, and one of the things it explained was why the leading physicians of the Arab world advocated eating yoghurt. They recommended it for dysentry and swellings of the stomach because it destroyed poisons in the intestine.

Hippocrates and Galen also held that yoghurt purified a burning and bilious stomach. Galen said that milk taken straight from the cow could cause the stomach to become inflamed, whereas fermented milk would not. Modern experiments confirm that yoghurt is more digestible than milk, within an hour of consumption, 96% of yoghurt is digested, as compared to only 32% of milk. Rahere, the physician who founded St Bartholomew's Hospital in London, also recommended yoghurt for health. He said it was 'refreshing to those in whose stomachs milk curdled, and in whose minds it caused heaviness and anxiety'.

Gandhi, who studied nutrition in London and

experimented with different methods of cooking with many foods that were not already a part of India's diet, pointed out that yoghurt was a cheap and easily accessible source of protein. He wrote a book called *Diet Reform* with the aim of introducing the poor of India, who could not afford to feed themselves properly, to foods that were cheap, or free, and naturally available. He suggested making jam with the skins of oranges, which would normally have been thrown away. He observed which leaves animals ate, and tried these in salads to see if they were palatable and, more importantly, he devoted a whole chapter of his book to yoghurt, skimmed milk, buttermilk and the sweetmeats made from them.

Perhaps the most famous champion of yoghurt was France's King François I. He fell ill with a mysterious disease which his doctors could neither

diagnose nor cure. He was wasting away when a man who had arrived from Constantinople came to the court offering a magic cure from his homeland. He fed the King on the solidified milk of goats. François made a miraculous recovery, paid the man a handsome fee for his 'secret' and continued eating yoghurt until the day he died. Ever since that time it has been known in France as *le lait de la vie eternelle*, the milk of eternal life.

NUTRITIONAL VALUE OF YOGHURT

Yoghurt is a wholesome and versatile food; the plain variety contains all the nutrients of the milk from which it was made, plus those from the added dried skimmed milk. Some yoghurts are fortified with vitamins A and D. When fruit and sugar are added, the mix is diluted, but its nutritional value remains roughly the same because of the extra milk solids needed to keep the fruit in suspension.

Yoghurt is given to hospital patients not only because it is nutritious and easily consumed by invalids, but because the live bacteria in it quickly replace the natural flora in the intestines that have been destroyed by the taking of antibiotics.

Yoghurt is also highly recommended for babies being weaned onto a solid diet, as it provides all the nutrients of milk in a more solid form and its organisms are very similar to those already in the baby's digestive tract. One way to discourage a child's sweet tooth is to feed an infant plain yoghurt or plain yoghurt mixed with fresh fruit purée, a healthy alternative to a sweetened dessert.

Anyone who is slimming will find yoghurt an invaluable part of their calorie-controlled diet. Plain yoghurt made with skimmed or semi-skimmed milk and reduced calorie yoghurt both supply a wide range of nutrients and are very low in calories. A 5 oz (150 g) tub (single serving) of low fat plain yoghurt contains 78 calories, and the same quantity of low fat fruit yoghurt provides 142 calories.

COMPOSITION OF YOGHURT
(LOW FAT):
GRAMS PER 3½ oz (100 g)

NUTRIENT	PLAIN	FLAVOURED	FRUIT	HAZELNUT
Water	85·7	79·0	74·9	73·4
Lactose	4·6	4·8	3·3	3·2
Other sugars	1·6a	9·2b	14·6b	13·3b
Protein	5·0	5·0	4·8	5·2
Fat	1·0	0·9	1·0	2·6
Minerals	0·8	0·8	0·8	0·8
Kilocalories per 100 g	52	81	95	106
Kilojoules per 100 g	216	342	405	449

a: Galactose
b: Mainly sucrose

Source: McCance and Widdowson's *The Composition of Foods*, 4th revised edition, by AA Paul and DAT Southgate (1978)

Yoghurt is a particularly good source of calcium and also contains iron, vitamin A, thiamin, riboflavin, niacin and ascorbic acid.

YOGHURT TODAY

Yoghurt is a booming business in Britain. In 1985 the nation consumed a record 1,175 million pots of it, or about 6½ lb (3 kg) per head of the population. However, we are still far behind France, West Germany and the Netherlands, where as early as 1973 consumption was respectively 8·6, 4·8 and 11·2 kg per head.

Though yoghurt has been sold in the UK for 60 years, it has only enjoyed large-scale popularity in the last 20, since the introduction of fruit yoghurt. The British are on the whole not keen on the tart flavour of traditional yoghurt. About 90% of the yoghurt sold is flavoured with fruit and sugar. These additions, plus the selective and controlled use of lactic acid-producing bacteria, have resulted in a bland product which is very much to the British taste.

Apart from the introduction of fruit and sugar, there have been other changes in the constituents of commercial yoghurt over recent years. Skimmed or partly skimmed milk has largely replaced whole milk as the basic ingredient. Dried skimmed milk is often added, as are flavours, colours, stabilisers and preservatives. All these things must be listed by law on the packaging. These additions and new technology have increased the range of yoghurts available to include drinking yoghurt, dried yoghurt, frozen yoghurt, whipped yoghurt and yoghurt heat-treated after fermentation to prolong shelf life.

Live v Sterilised Yoghurt

The point of heat-treating yoghurt after fermentation is that it destroys virtually all the lactic acid-producing bacteria, which means that it can be stored for longer without the addition of preservatives. While this is an advantage, many would argue that *Lactobacillus bulgaricus* and *Streptococcus thermophilus* are not only essential to the production of yoghurt, but that they should still be viable when the yoghurt is eaten. It is, after all, the living organisms in yoghurt that are responsible for its reputation as a health food.

The manufacturers who continue to produce live yoghurt contend that any product which does not contain living bacteria should not be described as yoghurt. As one of them says: 'Long life means no life.' They do have a point. But in many cases there is no difference in taste, texture or appearance between live and heat-treated yoghurt, and according to the Department of Health and Social Security, at least, no special nutritional or medical benefits can be derived from the live organisms in yoghurt anyway. The Ministry of Agriculture, Fisheries and Food, the body responsible for legislation on such subjects, took all these factors into account when it allowed the heat-treated product to be described as 'yoghurt'. It did add, however, that to alert the discriminating customer to the fact that this type of yoghurt contains few, if any, live bacteria, it should be labelled 'pasteurised' or 'sterilised'.

GREEK YOGHURT

One manufacturer who believes that yoghurt should always be live and never contain any additives such as colouring or preservatives has recently launched a Greek-style yoghurt made from cows' milk to compete with the imported Greek sheeps' milk yoghurts. Greek yoghurt is becoming increasingly popular because it is rich, smooth and creamy. It has a much more luxurious taste than low-fat yoghurt, while still being an entirely natural product. The reason for this is that it is made with 9% cream.

THE MANUFACTURE OF YOGHURT

The processes involved in the production of yoghurt vary slightly from one manufacturer to another, but roughly, this is what happens. The basic material is almost always skimmed or partly skimmed cows' milk. Milk is skimmed by spinning in a separator at a very high speed – 5,000–6,000 rpm. The centrifugal force separates the heavier skim milk, draining it to the outside of the container, while the cream is left at the axis of the spin in the centre.

The milk is then concentrated by evaporation, or by the addition of up to 6% dried skimmed milk. This process improves the consistency of the yoghurt, prevents the separation of whey and helps hold the pieces of fruit in suspension in fruit yoghurt.

The fat content of the mix can be increased by the addition of milk, cream or butter fat. The mix is then heated to about 160°F/70°C and homogenised to give it an even, creamy texture. To homogenise milk, it is forced at high pressure through a small aperture. This breaks the fat up into smaller globules, which remain evenly suspended in the milk.

The next step is to heat the mix for anything between 15 and 30 minutes to a temperature of 185–195°F/80–90°C, after which it is cooled to 115°F/45°C. The heat treatment pasteurises the basic mix and creates favourable conditions for the bacteria to multiply. *Lactobacillus bulgaricus* and *Streptococcus thermophilus* are now added in the form of a liquid culture. Very little is needed, just 1–3% of the volume of the mix.

The mix is then incubated at 105–115°F/40–45°C, so that the bacteria multiply rapidly and fermentation takes place. The bacteria convert the lactose in the milk into lactic acid. This sours the milk, causing its casein content to coagulate and form the texture of yoghurt. Fermentation takes from 2–4 hours and constant checks are made during this period so that the yoghurt has the desired acidity. The lactic acid content of yoghurt in the United Kingdom is only about 1.5%, as the sourer products from Eastern Europe are not popular in this country.

Fermentation can take place in large vats or in the tubs in which the yoghurt will be sold. Vat-fermented yoghurt needs a longer incubation period and is stirred before being transferred to tubs. It is viscous and fluid and usually referred to as stirred yoghurt. The yoghurt fermented in the tubs is of the set variety. The difference is obvious as soon as you open the pot.

STORAGE

Once the yoghurt has reached the right acidity, it is cooled and stored at below 40°F/5°C to prevent further fermentation. It is kept at this temperature until it is sold, and has a recommended shelf life of about 15 days. After about 30 days the bacteria may multiply sufficiently to increase the acid level to a point where it becomes unpalatable to most people in this country. Ultimately the bacteria will die and the yoghurt will separate into a shrunken solid curd with liquid whey round the sides and on the surface.

Whey may appear at any stage in a perfectly fresh set yoghurt if the container is knocked or shaken. Although this affects the appearance of the product, there is no loss of flavour or food value. The yoghurt can be stirred before being eaten.

THE ADDITION OF FRUIT

Real fruit yoghurt is usually made with stirred yoghurt. Extra dried skimmed milk and small quantities of stabilisers may be added to hold the fruit in suspension and the fruit is added when the yoghurt is transferred to the tubs. Obviously great care must be taken to ensure that the fruit does not start to ferment itself, which would give rise to yeasts and moulds growing in the yoghurt. For this reason, fresh or frozen fruit is pasteurised before use, or canned fruit may be used.

Many fruit yoghurts also contain colourings, flavourings and sugar, which can be added before fermentation. There are even set yoghurts which contain colourings, flavourings and sugar, but no fruit.

YOGHURT AROUND THE WORLD

Yoghurt can be, and is, made from the milk of any animal, not just the cow. Egyptologists have discovered that as long ago as 3000BC the Egyptians kept tame herds of antelope and gazelle, and ancient Egyptian paintings show milking in progress: the animal's hind legs were tied and one worker held onto a foreleg while another did the milking. Since the Pharaohs ate yoghurt at their banquets, it is reasonable to assume that it was made from the milk of antelope and gazelle.

The flavour of yoghurt depends not only on the type of milk used, but also on the cultures intro-duced into it, which vary slightly from one part of the world to another, and the length of fermentation. In Britain, America and Western Europe, yoghurt is bland and creamy, but elsewhere it is sour, bubbling and alcoholic. Where the fermentation produces only lactic acid from lactose, as in the Western production of yoghurt, the term homofermentation is used, whereas when the end products are lactic acid, alcohol and carbon dioxide, as for example in the *kefir* of Russia, the process is known as heterofermentation.

In Tibet, yoghurt is made from yaks' milk, and in Lapland from the milk of reindeer. In South Russia, the Caucasus and Central Asia, yoghurt is made from mares' milk and the bacteria introduced produce a bubbling acidic brew with a high alcohol content. The yoghurt is fermented in sealed bottles and the result is effervescent. A similar product is made in Chile, where it is known as 'whey champagne'. The most alcoholic yoghurt of all comes from Turkestan and contains an astonishing 7.1% alcohol!

In the Middle East, where yoghurt is called 'leben' or 'laban', it is made from the milk of goats, cows and buffaloes and sometimes fermented by the addition of yeast. In parts of the Sahara, where the basic ingredient is, of course, camels' milk, the yoghurt starter is often a piece of decaying vegetable or animal matter – or it can be the bacteria present in the vessel holding the milk. Though this sounds dangerous, it has been proved that bacteria which might be harmful if consumed in milk are destroyed by the lactic acid in yoghurt. This is the reason why, when travelling in hot countries, it is always safer to eat the yoghurt than to drink the milk.

WHAT
YOGHURT
IS CALLED
AROUND
THE WORLD

Armenia – *matzoon, mazun*

Balkans – *tarho*

Burma – *tyre*

Bulgaria – *yaourt*

Carpathians – *urda*

Chile – *skuta*

East Carpathians – *huslanka*

Egypt, Sudan – *zababy, zabade*

Far East – *saya*

Finland – *plimae*

Greece – *tiaourti*

Hungary – *tako*

Iceland – *skyr*

India – *dahi*

Iran – *mast*

Iraq, Lebanon, Egypt – *leben, laban*

Lapland – *pauira*

Norway – *kaelder-milk*

Saudi Arabia – *laban raid*

Scandinavia – *taeffe*

Siberia – *koumiss*

Sicily – *mezzorada*

South Russia and the Caucasus – *kefir, kuban*

Sudan, Iraq – *roba, rob*

Turkestan – *busa*

Curdled milk solidified forms a major part of the diet of many African tribes. The Zulus eat it as a wet cheese seasoned with salt and pepper.

The Oxford English Dictionary lists more than 10 ways of spelling yoghurt: the most common alternatives in the UK are *yogurt* and *yoghourt*.

THE MAGICAL POWERS OF YOGHURT

Eating yoghurt bestows long life – or immortality, depending on which country and which century you come from. The people of the Caucasus traditionally attribute it with other powers besides. They say that:

* Flavoured with garlic it can cure tuberculosis.

* Taken neat, it restores hair to bald heads.

* If consumed before and after a binge, it will avert a hangover.

* And when eaten by lovers it will act as an aphrodisiac.

During the First World War, yoghurt was found to be very useful among the British troops abroad suffering from dysentery when administered as an enema.

The positive action of the live bacteria in yoghurt has also prompted modern doctors to recommend it as a douche for thrush, and it can soothe the irritation and cure the complaint in cases where all other remedies have failed.

Beauticians have not neglected the possibilities of yoghurt as a treatment for hair and skin.

* It can be rubbed into the hair after a shampoo to get rid of dandruff.

* It can be smeared on to the face straight out of the pot; it soothes and cleanses the skin, leaving it feeling fresh and relaxed.

* A more vigorous face mask can be made with a little yoghurt, some crushed oats and mashed raspberries. If you can resist eating this, massage it into your face (the grittiness of the oats tones the skin) and leave for 10 minutes before splashing off with cold water. No doubt this is the sort of facial that Cleopatra enjoyed while she was lounging in her bath of asses' milk!

MAKING YOGHURT
AT HOME

Yoghurt is very easy and cheap to make at home. All you need is milk and a starter, and the starter can be commercial plain yoghurt. You can also buy a dried starter containing the two bacteria needed to make yoghurt. If you buy the commercial product instructions will be supplied with it. If you use ordinary yoghurt, proceed as follows.

1. Heat 1 pint (600 ml) sterilised or UHT milk to 110°F/43°C, which is approximately blood heat if you have no thermometer. Alternatively, boiled and cooled pasteurised milk may be used.

2. Blend in 1 level tablespoon plain yoghurt, and 2 oz (50 g) dried skimmed milk (optional).

3. Transfer the mix to a bowl, cover with a plate and leave in a warm place, such as the airing cupboard, for about 10 hours until yoghurt has formed.

4. Put the yoghurt in the refrigerator and leave for a further 4 hours to thicken further before eating.

* Remember to keep a spoonful of this yoghurt back to make your next batch.

* Home-made yoghurt will keep for up to about five days, covered, in the fridge.

* Make a richer product by substituting 2 oz (50 g) dried whole milk powder for the skimmed milk or by adding a dollop of cream.

* It is important that any equipment used should be scrupulously cleaned beforehand by immersing in boiling water or a commercial sterilising solution.

YOGHURT DRINKS

Refreshing yoghurt drinks are enjoyed all over India and the Middle East, at home and in cafés or from the stalls of street vendors. The Persians call them *abdug*, the Lebanese call them *ayran*, and elsewhere they are known as *laban*.

LABAN

The easiest way to make *laban* is in a blender. The basic recipe mixes together 1 pint (600 ml) each yoghurt and water, a pinch of salt and about 2 tablespoons chopped fresh mint leaves.

LASSI

Lassi, the popular Indian drink, is made from equal quantities of yoghurt and water with crushed ice cubes and a pinch of salt added. This should be blended until frothy, poured into tall frosted glasses and sprinkled with toasted cumin seeds. The perfect cool accompaniment to a fiery curry!

YOGHURT SHAKES

The idea of a yoghurt drink can be thoroughly adapted to Western tastes in the making of yoghurt shakes. Blend together equal quantities of yoghurt (sweetened and with added fruit if you like) and milk. If using plain yoghurt, add some chopped fresh fruit or fruit purée. Yoghurt shakes can be sprinkled with chopped or slivered nuts or desiccated coconut.

DRINKS AND COCKTAILS

For a less rich drink, 2 measures of yoghurt can be blended with 1 measure each of fresh fruit or vegetable juice and sparkling mineral water. You can make a yoghurt cocktail by adding a splash of rum or fruit liqueur. The idea of yoghurt and alcohol may seem rather strange until you remember that in many countries yoghurt itself is alcoholic.

BREAKFAST-IN-A-GLASS

Blend together a single serving of yoghurt (5 oz/ 150 g tub) with the same quantity of orange juice, a raw egg, a pinch of mixed spice and 1 tablespoon clear honey. That should set you up for the day!

COOKING WITH YOGHURT

Yoghurt is an extremely versatile food, yet in the West it is still most common sweetened and fruit-flavoured and eaten as a dessert or a snack. In the Middle East, on the other hand, it is used as a topping for sweet or savoury dishes, as a marinade, in pastries, cakes, soups and stews. It complements all other foods – fruit, of course, but also vegetables, eggs, cheese, fish, meat and grains. It is the ideal food for slimmers, the very young, the very old, the sick and the health conscious.

Yoghurt is an excellent substitute for cream and can be used in place of it in most dishes to save on calories, cholesterol and cash, and to give a fresher taste.

Prolonged cooking at a high temperature will make it separate, which will spoil its appearance and change its texture. For this reason it is better to remove food from the heat before stirring in yoghurt. Alternatively, yoghurt can be stabilised by the addition of flour or egg, after which it can be boiled without spoiling.

STABILISING YOGHURT

Yoghurt can be stabilised by the addition of flour or egg. Either stir a dessertspoonful of cornflour into a little water and mix it with the yoghurt or beat an egg into the yoghurt. Then follow the recipe.

Stabilised and cooked yoghurt cannot be used as a starter because the heat will have killed the bacteria.

RECIPES

FISHERMAN'S DIP

Yoghurt is ideal for making dips, and this one comes from Cornwall. Serve it with sticks of celery and carrot, crunchy radishes, spring onions and crisp cauliflower florets – in fact any vegetable with a bite that's good to eat raw.

8 oz (225 g) smoked mackerel fillets
5 oz (150 g) curd cheese
1 tablespoon horseradish sauce
1–2 tablespoons lemon juice
5 oz (150 g) yoghurt
freshly ground pepper

Skin the fillets and flake the fish, removing any bones, then purée in a liquidiser. Mix with the curd cheese, horseradish sauce and lemon juice to taste, then beat in enough yoghurt to make a smooth consistency. Season with pepper.

GUACAMOLE

A delicious dip to serve with crudités or tortillas.

1 large ripe avocado
1 small onion, chopped
1 large tomato, skinned, deseeded and chopped
a dash of lime or lemon juice
5 oz (150 g) yoghurt
a pinch of chilli powder or ½ small fresh chilli, deseeded
and finely chopped

Cut the avocado in half and remove the stone. Scoop
the flesh from the shell and put in the liquidiser with
the onion, tomato and lime or lemon juice. Blend
until smooth. Transfer to a bowl, stir in the yoghurt
and sprinkle with chilli powder or chopped chilli.

RAITA

(YOGHURT RELISH)

A cooling accompaniment to a fiery curry.

½ cucumber, diced
salt
2 spring onions, chopped
1 clove of garlic, crushed
small bunch of fresh coriander leaves, chopped
5 oz (150 g) yoghurt

Sprinkle the cucumber with salt and leave for a while to 'sweat', then drain.

Mix the drained cucumber with the chopped spring onion, garlic, coriander and yoghurt. Chill for up to an hour before serving.

TSATSIKI

(YOGHURT SALAD)

You will nearly always find refreshing tsatsiki served as part of a Greek *mezze*. It makes an excellent dip or summer salad served with hot pitta bread.

1/2 pint (300 ml) yoghurt
1/2 small cucumber, peeled and diced
1 fat clove of garlic, finely sliced
few mint leaves, chopped
salt

To garnish:
paprika
mint leaves

Peel and chop the cucumber into tiny dice. Place in a sieve and leave for 30 minutes to drain.

Mix the cucumber with the remaining ingredients, adding salt to taste. Refrigerate for 1/2–1 hour and serve very cold, sprinkled with paprika and perhaps decorated with mint leaves.

CHICKEN AND ALMOND SOUP

This is a smooth, delicately flavoured soup from the Middle East that should be served warm, but not hot. Garnish with toasted flaked almonds or chopped chervil.

4 oz (100 g) ground almonds
4 hard-boiled egg yolks
1 pint (600 ml) chicken stock
1/4 pint (150 ml) milk
2 oz (50 g) cooked chicken, shredded
5 oz (150 g) yoghurt
salt
freshly ground black pepper

Mix the almonds and egg yolks to a paste with a little of the chicken stock.

Heat the remaining chicken stock with the milk and shredded chicken in a pan, and when hot blend a couple of spoonfuls into the almond paste. Add the almond mixture to the pan and heat through. Do not allow to boil.

When ready to serve, stir in the yoghurt. Check the seasoning and pour into warmed soup bowls.

Serves 4

ESHKENEH SHIRAZI

From the city of Shiraz in the heart of ancient Persia, this unusual and exotic soup can be served hot or icy cool in the summer. A perfect dinner party soup.

1 large onion, finely chopped
2 tablespoons butter
2 tablespoons flour
2 oz (50 g) walnuts, chopped
1 teaspoon ground fenugreek
2 pints (1.1 l) hot water
1 pint (600 ml) yoghurt
salt and pepper

Fry the onion in the butter over a very low heat until golden brown, and stir in the flour. Continue to cook, adding walnuts and fenugreek and, when well amalgamated, quickly beat in ½ cup of water. Gradually add remaining water and bring to the boil. Correct seasoning and simmer for 20 minutes.

Beat the yoghurt in a bowl until smooth. Stir in 1 cup of hot soup and gradually return mixture to soup. Heat through, taking care not to let the soup boil, as this will make it curdle, and serve immediately.

Serves 6–8

GAZPACHO

This soup should be served chilled, outdoors on a hot day. It makes an excellent slimmer's lunch.

1 green pepper, pith and seeds removed, diced
1 red pepper, pith and seeds removed, diced
1 large onion, chopped
4 Mediterranean tomatoes, skinned, deseeded
  and chopped
1 fat clove of garlic
½ pint (300 ml) tomato juice
10 oz (300 g) yoghurt
bread croûtons

Reserving a little of the diced peppers and chopped onion, put all the vegetables in the liquidiser with the tomato juice and blend until smooth. Tip into a large bowl, stir in the yoghurt until well mixed, then chill.

To serve, stir in some shattered ice cubes, then pour into individual bowls and garnish with the reserved diced vegetables and croûtons.

Serves 2–3

PRAWN, APPLE AND WALNUT COCKTAIL

Yoghurt makes a light and refreshing salad dressing and a healthy alternative to mayonnaise. Crumble a little blue cheese into it and mash with the back of a spoon to dress a celery salad, or toss in plenty of fresh chopped herbs and serve with fish. Or you can make this delicious tangy prawn cocktail.

10 oz (300 g) yoghurt
2 tablespoons lemon juice
salt and freshly ground pepper
2 rosy skinned apples
8 oz (225 g) prawns
3 oz (75 g) walnut pieces

In a bowl, stir together the yoghurt and lemon juice and add seasoning to taste. Core the apples, but do not peel, and slice them into the dressing. Stir to coat.

Peel all but 4 of the prawns and toss them into the salad with the walnut pieces. Divide between 4 individual dishes and garnish each with a prawn.

Serves 4

BEEF STROGANOFF

This classic dish is too rich for many people when cooked in the traditional way with heavy cream.

1½ lb (750 g) fillet steak
black pepper
4 oz (100 g) butter
4 oz (100 g) onions, sliced
6 oz (175 g) mushrooms, sliced
5 oz (150 g) yoghurt
1 tablespoon dry sherry
salt and pepper

Cut the steak into strips about 2 inches (5 cm) long and season with pepper.

Heat half the butter and fry the onions until golden brown. Remove with a slotted spoon and keep warm.

Add the mushrooms to the pan and fry gently until tender. Add to the onions and keep warm.

Add the remaining butter to the pan, increase the heat and fry the steak quickly in two batches for about 3 minutes each side. Keep the first batch warm with the vegetables while you fry the second.

Return all the meat and vegetables to the pan, shake over the heat, then add most of the yoghurt and sherry and seasoning. Heat through without boiling and serve on a bed of rice with the remaining yoghurt swirled on top.

Serves 4

GOULASCH

A traditional winter favourite from Hungary. Serve it with boiled or baked potatoes.

2 tablespoons oil
1 lb (450 g) braising steak, trimmed and cubed
2 teaspoons paprika
1 tablespoon flour
1/2 pint (300 ml) beef stock
8 oz (225 g) onions, sliced
8 oz (225 g) carrots, sliced
14 oz (400 g) can tomatoes, mashed with juice
juice of 1/2 lemon
salt and freshly ground pepper
5 oz (150 g) yoghurt
2 tablespoons chopped chives

Heat the oven to 300°F/150°C/Gas 3.

Heat the oil in a pan and fry the meat briskly on all sides to brown and seal in the juices. Add the paprika and flour and cook for a couple of minutes, stirring. Gradually add the stock and stir to thicken. Transfer the contents of the pan to a casserole.

Put the onions and carrots in the pan, cover and sweat over gentle heat until the onion is transparent. Stir in the tomatoes, lemon juice and seasoning. Heat through, then stir into the casserole, cover and cook for 1½ hours until the meat is tender.

To serve, spoon on yoghurt and sprinkle with chives.

Serves 4

SAG GOSHT

One of India's best-loved dishes – and a curry restaurant favourite – combines spiced lamb and spinach with cooling yoghurt.

1½ lb (750 g) lamb, cubed
2 cloves of garlic, crushed
2 teaspoons grated fresh ginger
1 teaspoon ground turmeric
½ teaspoon chilli powder
3 tablespoons oil
2 medium onions, thinly sliced
1 inch (2.5 cm) cinnamon stick
4 cardamom pods
1½ lb (700 g) fresh spinach, washed, drained and roughly chopped
5 oz (150 g) yoghurt

Put the lamb in a dish and add the garlic, ginger, turmeric and chilli powder. Turn to coat, cover and leave in a cool place for 2 hours.

Heat the oil in a pan, add the onions, cinnamon and cardamoms and fry for 3–4 minutes. Add the meat and fry briskly on all sides to seal. Turn down the heat, stir in the spinach and yoghurt, cover and cook gently for about 45 minutes until the meat is tender.

Serve hot with rice.

Serves 4

CHICKEN KORMA

This is a mild fragrant curry and will be enjoyed even by those who don't normally like spicy food. Traditionally a korma is very rich; meat, chicken or vegetables are cooked in yoghurt and spiced with saffron and other aromatic spices. Sometimes it is sprinkled with chopped almonds.

4 chicken pieces
about 2 tablespoons oil for frying
1 clove of garlic, chopped
1 onion, thinly sliced
4 cardamom pods
1 inch (2.5 cm) cinnamon stick

For the marinade:
5 oz (150 g) yoghurt
1 teaspoon turmeric
1 clove of garlic, crushed

Wash the chicken and dry on absorbent paper. Mix the ingredients for the marinade thoroughly and coat the chicken in it. Leave for 1–2 hours to absorb the flavours.

Heat the oven to 300°F/150°C/Gas 2.

Heat the oil in a pan, add the garlic, onion and spices and fry gently until the onion is golden. Transfer to a casserole, add the chicken and the marinade, cover and cook for 1½ hours until tender.

Serve with rice.

Serves 4

PANCAKES

You can make very good pancake batter with yoghurt, and it is excellent too for light fillings of chicken, fish, spinach, asparagus and, of course, fruit.

For the batter:
4 oz (100 g) plain flour
a pinch of salt
1 egg
¼ pint (150 ml) water
5 oz (150 g) yoghurt

For a savoury filling:
per pancake, you will need 1 tablespoon each of:
curd cheese,
yoghurt and cooked chicken
or flaked smoked haddock or tuna
or cooked spinach, well drained and chopped
or 1 or 2 asparagus spears, cooked until tender

For a sweet filling:
per pancake, you will need 1 tablespoon each of:
curd cheese, yoghurt and cooked or fresh fruit purée
    mixed with a little grated orange rind
a squeeze of lemon juice and a sprinkling of caster sugar
fresh fruit to garnish

Sieve the flour and salt into a bowl. Make a well in the middle and add the egg with half the water. Beat until smooth. Gradually beat in the remaining water mixed with the yoghurt. Cover the bowl and leave the batter to rest for 30 minutes.

Lightly oil a heavy-based pan and cook the batter a spoonful at a time, frying gently on both sides until spotted golden brown. You should have about 8 pancakes. Keep them warm as you make them.

Divide the filling between the pancakes, roll them up and heat through briefly in a warm oven, or in a microwave for 1–2 minutes if you have one.

Serve immediately.

Serves 4

PASTA WITH CHEESE AND HERBS

This is a quick and very simple dish that tastes equally good hot or cold, so any leftovers can be eaten as a salad. Yoghurt creamed with blue cheese makes another good pasta sauce.

14 oz (400 g) tagliatelle verde, fresh if possible

For the sauce:
4 oz (100 g) curd cheese
1 clove of garlic, crushed
a handful of fresh herbs chopped, such as basil, parsley, mint, chervil
5 oz (150 g) yoghurt

To serve:
2 oz (50 g) grated parmesan

First make the sauce by creaming together all the ingredients. Season with salt and freshly ground black pepper if liked.

Cook the pasta in plenty of boiling salted water, to which you have added 1 teaspoon oil. Fresh pasta will take only 2 minutes. If using dried pasta, follow the instructions on the packet.

Drain the pasta, toss in the sauce and serve sprinkled with parmesan cheese.

Serves 4

COURGETTE QUICHE

You can use yoghurt instead of cream when making a quiche, which immediately makes it a healthier and less fattening dish. Any quiche recipe can be adapted – the one below uses young courgettes that don't need to be pre-cooked.

8 oz (225 g) shortcrust pastry
4 eggs
10 oz (300 g) yoghurt
3 oz (75 g) grated parmesan
salt
freshly ground pepper
grated nutmeg
1¼ lb (625 g) baby courgettes, sliced
1 tablespoon brown breadcrumbs

Line a flan tin with pastry, making sure that it stands about ½ inch (1 cm) above the rim. Prick the base with a fork and bake blind at 400°F/200°C/Gas 6 for 10–15 minutes.

Meanwhile, beat together the eggs, yoghurt and 2 oz (50 g) grated parmesan and season to taste with salt and pepper. Stir in a pinch of nutmeg.

Put the courgettes into the pastry case and pour over the yoghurt mixture. Mix the remaining cheese with the breadcrumbs and sprinkle on top. Return to the oven for 30–40 minutes until puffy and golden.

Serves 4

YOGURTLU PATATES

This Balkan speciality is as light as a soufflé and delicious served as a main course or as an accompaniment to all roasts.

2 lb (1 kg) potatoes, peeled, boiled and drained
4 tablespoons yoghurt
1 tablespoon butter
2 eggs, separated
1 tablespoon chopped chives
1/2 teaspoon dried thyme
1/4 teaspoon paprika
pinch of nutmeg
salt and pepper

Mash the potatoes together with the butter and yoghurt until creamy. Beat in the egg yolks with all the herbs and seasoning. Whisk the egg whites until stiff and gradually fold into the potato mixture. Gently pour the mixture into a lightly buttered soufflé dish and sprinkle with nutmeg.

Cook soufflé for 25–30 minutes in an oven preheated to 350°F/180°C/Gas 4. Serve immediately.

Serves 4–6

MIDDLE EASTERN SALAD

Yoghurt is as much prized today as ever in the Middle East for its digestive qualities, and is often served with hot or cold vegetables. You can give this salad a Greek flavour by adding cubes of feta cheese, halved black olives and a sprinkling of chopped chilli.

1 green pepper, pith and seeds removed, thinly sliced
1 large onion, thinly sliced into rings
3 Mediterranean tomatoes, cut up coarsely
a handful of radishes, sliced
1/2 cucumber, peeled and cut into chunks
1 very crisp lettuce, cut into manageable pieces

For the dressing:
5 oz (150 g) yoghurt
1 tablespoon olive oil
1 tablespoon lemon juice
1 clove of garlic, crushed
2 tablespoons fresh chopped mint
salt
plenty of freshly ground pepper

Mix the salad ingredients together in a large bowl. Mix the ingredients for the dressing in a separate bowl, then pour over the salad and toss well.

Serve with crusty bread.

Serves 4

SPICED YOGHURT WITH BANANAS

Traditionally served as an accompaniment to curries and kebabs, this substantial dish is also delicious as a snack, spread generously on a chapati or on hot pitta bread.

½ pint (300 ml) yoghurt
3 firm bananas, peeled and sliced
3 tablespoons desiccated coconut, moistened with a little water
2 tablespoons lemon juice
½ teaspoon salt
pinch chilli powder
2 teaspoons vegetable oil
½ teaspoon each of cumin and black mustard seeds

Combine the yoghurt with bananas, coconut, lemon juice. Season with salt and chilli powder to taste.

Heat oil in a small saucepan and fry the cumin and black mustard seeds until the mustard pops. Fold this into the yoghurt and serve.

Serves 4

PEACH SOUFFLÉ

Decorated with pistachio nuts or slices of peach.

1/2 oz (15 g) powdered gelatine
3 tablespoons water
3 eggs, separated
2 oz (50 g) caster sugar
10 oz (300 g) yoghurt
1 fresh peach, skinned and puréed

Dissolve the gelatine in the water. Whisk the egg yolks and sugar until thick and fluffy, then beat in the yoghurt and peach purée.

In a separate bowl, beat the egg whites until stiff.

Add the gelatine to the yoghurt mixture. As soon as it starts to set, carefully fold in the egg whites – do not beat or stir. Tip the mixture into a buttered soufflé dish and chill until set.

Serves 4

BLACKBERRY YOGHURT BRÛLÉE

This is a lighter alternative to crème caramel – another demonstration of the amazing versatility of yoghurt.

10 oz (300 g) yoghurt
4 oz (100 g) ripe blackberries, mashed to a pulp
3 egg yolks
1 oz (25 g) vanilla sugar
2 oz (50 g) demerara sugar

Heat the oven to 325°F/160°C/Gas 3.

Stir the yoghurt and the blackberries together until smooth, and beat in the egg yolks and vanilla sugar. Divide between 4 ovenproof cocotte dishes. Set the dishes in a roasting tin half-filled with hot water. Place in the oven for 25–30 minutes, until set.

Preheat the grill to very hot.

Sprinkle the tops of the cocottes with a generous layer of sugar and put under the grill until it melts and turns to golden caramel.

Allow to cool and chill for 2–3 hours before serving.

Serves 4

BANANA CAKE

This dark and deliciously moist cake can be eaten for breakfast thickly spread with butter or curd cheese. It is exceptionally easy to make and keeps well.

8 oz (225 g) wholemeal flour
a pinch of salt
2 teaspoons baking powder
2 tablespoons arachide oil (or any tasteless oil)
2 oz (50 g) butter or polyunsaturated margarine, softened
4 tablespoons runny honey
2 or 3 bananas, mashed
3oz (75 g) yoghurt

Preheat the oven to 350°F/175°C/Gas 4.
    Mix the flour, salt and baking powder together. In a separate bowl, beat the remaining ingredients together until smooth and fluffy. Combine the two. Pour into a greased and floured loaf tin and bake for about 1 hour, until a cocktail stick stuck into the cake comes out clean. Allow to cool on a wire rack.

CINNAMON TARTS

These can be served hot from the oven as a dessert, or allowed to cool and eaten at teatime. Soak the raisins in water first to plump them up.

8 oz (225 g) shortcrust pastry
2 eggs
1 oz (25 g) sugar
1 oz (25 g) plain flour
a pinch powdered cinnamon
5 oz (150 g) yoghurt
2 oz (50 g) raisins

Use the pastry to line 6 individual tart tins. Bake blind at 400°F/200°C/Gas 6 for 10–15 minutes until set.

Whisk the eggs with the sugar until thick and fluffy. Sift the flour and cinnamon into the yoghurt and stir to blend. Fold this into the egg mixture.

Pour the filling into the tart cases and return to the oven, reducing the heat to 350°F/180°C/Gas 4, for 10 minutes. Top with the raisins and return to the oven for 10 minutes, until golden.

Makes 6

STRAWBERRY ICE CREAM

This very sumptuous ice cream, made with only natural ingredients, tastes wholly unlike the commercial variety. Serve topped with whole fresh strawberries.

6 oz (175 g) fresh strawberries
2 tablespoons skimmed milk powder
4 tablespoons runny honey
5 oz (150 g) yoghurt
¼ pint (150 ml) double cream

Put the strawberries in the liquidiser with the milk powder and honey and purée until smooth. Stir in the yoghurt and freeze until firm but not solid.
    Beat the mixture until smooth. Whip the cream and fold into the fruit. Freeze until firm.

Serves 4

YOGHURT LOLLIES

To make yoghurt lollies, mix a little fruit purée into yoghurt and freeze in lolly moulds.

LOGANBERRY YOGHURT SORBET

Make this dessert with any soft fruit in season. Really ripe berries can be squashed with a fork to make a purée, or you can press them through a sieve with the back of a spoon or blend in a liquidiser.

8 oz (225 g) loganberry purée, plus a few
*   berries for decoration*
10 oz (300 g) yoghurt
juice of 1/2 lemon
2 oz (50 g) caster sugar
1/2 oz (15 g) powdered gelatine
2 egg whites

Put the loganberry purée in a bowl and stir in the yoghurt and lemon juice. Sweeten to taste with sugar.

Put 4 tablespoons cold water in a small bowl and sprinkle on the gelatine. Leave to stand for 5 minutes. Set the bowl over a pan of hot water and stir until the gelatine has dissolved and the liquid is clear. Stir into the loganberry mixture.

In a separate bowl, beat the egg whites until stiff, then carefully fold them into the purée. Cover and put in the freezing compartment of the fridge.

When almost frozen, beat the mixture with a rotary whisk. Divide between 4 individual dishes and freeze until set.

Serve decorated with fresh loganberries.

Serves 4

YOGHURT CHEESE (LABNA)

Labna is a delicious yoghurt cheese served for breakfast, or as an hors d'oeuvre in the Middle East sprinkled with chopped herbs and olive oil. To make it, first make your yoghurt. Then line a colander or sieve with muslin and stand it in a bowl or in the sink to allow the whey to drain off. Put the yoghurt in the muslin and wait for about 6 hours until the creamy crumbly cheese has formed.

PANEER

(INDIAN CHEESE)

One way of serving paneer is fried with peas, chopped parsley and a little cayenne pepper and turmeric – this makes Mattar Paneer, which is quite delicious.

2 pints (1 litre) milk
1 teaspoon alum (available from a chemist)

Boil the milk, remove from the heat and stir in the alum. Return the pan to the heat and continue to cook, stirring, until the milk curdles and separates completely. Drain in a colander, then put the cheese in a muslin bag and squeeze all the moisture out of it. It will be crumbly like dry scrambled eggs.

PROUST'S DELIGHT

In Proust's great epic, *À la recherche du temps perdu*, he describes the delight of eating a simple dessert of fresh cream cheese into which he would crush strawberries to make it pink. The type of cheese he would have eaten, made on the farms of the Loire Valley, is not dry and crumbly like the cream cheese than can be bought commercially. It is richer, smoother and tangier – in fact, more like a mixture of yoghurt, goats' cheese and double cream. To make it at home, mash a small fresh goats' cheese (about 4 oz/100 g) into 1 lb (450 g) yoghurt. Whip 5 oz/150 g double cream and fold it in. For a truly Proustian delight, serve it crushed with strawberries to give it the soft pink of hawthorn blossoms:

'Just look at this pink one; isn't it pretty?' And it
was indeed a hawthorn, but one whose flowers
were pink, and lovelier even than the white . . . it
was attired even more richly than the rest, for the
flowers which clung to its branches, one above
another, so thickly as to leave no part of the tree
undecorated, like the tassels wreathed about the
crook of a rococo shepherdess, were every one of
them 'in colour' and consequently of a superior
quality, by the aesthetic standards of Combray, to
the 'plain', if one was to judge by the scale of
prices at the 'stores' in the Square, or at Camus's,
where the most expensive biscuits were those
whose sugar was pink. And for my own part I set
a higher value on cream cheese when it was pink,
when I had been allowed to tinge it with crushed
strawberries. And these flowers had chosen pre-
cisely the colour of some edible and delicious
thing . . .'

ACKNOWLEDGEMENTS

The author would like to thank the following people and organisations for their help:

Yoxford Post Office and Natural Food Stores; DW Mersh, Bailey Milk Products Ltd; Daphne Holloway, Loseley; NJ Hunter, Eden Vale; JD Cranston, Kennerty Farm Dairies Ltd; Ministry of Agriculture, Fisheries and Foods; Janet Nunn, Creamery Proprietors' Association; Kathy Cuddihy, St Ivel; Tullia Waddell, Dairy Crest; Anne Stacey, National Dairy Council.

For further reading: Arto der Haroutunian's *The Yoghurt Book* (Penguin); PE Norris's *About Yoghurt* (Thorsons).